ISBN # **9798731641432**

Contents

How to make money when you are broke?

Do you often feel that you never have *enough* money?Are you that teenager in your friend circle who has to avoid going to clubs and parties because you don't have money? Are you that kid in class who constantly gets sidelined just because you're pocket money seems to get over even before you know it? Do you want the latest i-phone but lost all your savings when you hosted that stupid high school party?

Are you that 20-something whose monthly salary ends before the next one comes? Have you lost count of people you owe money to? Do you have to constantly choose between paying the rent and buying your kid his birthday gift? Are you so debt-laden that the only thing on your mind is what to sell next?

Are you that retired citizen whose pension doesn't let you live the kind of life you want to? Is your retirement corpus on a threateningly low level that you can't manage to watch a single game once in a while?

Then yes, my friend, you might not like to hear it, but you are BROKE! School / tuition fees, food, traveling, clothing, grocery, personal hygiene, house rent, internet bill, phone bill, electricity charges and what not!

If there is one source of earning money, there are at least 10 needs of spending it. But relax my friend; you're not the only person in the world that's going through this. A lot of great people have been in such situations; in fact, more dire situations, but have defied all odds to see the light on the other side of the tunnel. Always remember if there is a problem that exists there is a solution that exists too.

The right attitude .....

Here's a thing about being broke, if you feel you have already hit the rock-bottom you also know there's only way up now. In such situations, it's very important to have the right attitude. Dave Ramsey, author of the book, **"The Total Money Makeover: A Proven Plan for Financial Fitness"**, summed it up perfectly by saying, ***"Winning at money is 80 percent behavior and 20 percent head knowledge. What to do isn't the problem; doing it is. Most of us know what to do, but we just don't do it. If I can control the guy in the mirror, I can be skinny and rich."***

At this point of time you know that you are running out of money, that you need to cut down on your expenses, and that you need to get a job to make some money. That's about it. Stop right there. You don't need to think too much. If those thoughts have already crossed your mind, you are done with thinking. It is time to act. Too much of thinking will lead you nowhere. Overthinking might make you depressed, sad, anxious, guilty and what not. The more you think, the tougher it is going to get for you come out of it.

Napoleon Hill, author of 'Think and Grow Rich' talked about how important it is to not get caught with emotional turmoil in such situations. He said ***"Don't take it too seriously, no matter what it is. During the Depression, I had four of my friends commit suicide. Two of them jumped off tall buildings, one shot himself, and another one took poison. They did it because they lost all their money. I lost twice as much as they did, but I didn't jump off any building, I didn't shoot myself, I didn't poison myself ... My mental attitude towards it was to start looking for that seed of improvement ."***

The author also stresses on how important it is to take initiative and get into action instead of sitting and whining about your fate. He keeps it simple, ***"You don't have to be very brilliant. You don't have to have such a wonderful education. You can be an outstanding success if you will only take what little you have, whether it's little or a lot, and start using it, putting it into action, do something about it, and do something with it. And, of course, that calls for an initiative. "*** If you get a chance you should definitely read this book. It will surely help you build the right attitude when it comes to money making and success.

And you never know what you'll end up discovering along the way of making ends meet! If you study lives of great inventors and businessmen you will realize almost all of them struggled to make ends meet at some or the other point of time in their lives. As they say, ***'necessity is the mother of invention.'*** Their need to earn money led to some great inventions that the world is thankful for today.

Take the example of Samuel Walton, American Entrepreneur who started the famous Walmart store (chain of grocery and general stores.) He milked the family cow, bottled the milk and drove it to the customers. Afterwards, he also started delivering newspapers along the way and sold magazine subscriptions. That is how he supported his poor family while in school. The man was broke because he was poor, not because of any mistake. It was his fate. But instead of getting dejected he found ways of making money right from his childhood. While in college he would wait the tables in exchange for meals. At the age of 26, he took a loan to start a small grocery store which became extremely successful in three years. So the first thing he did was to step out of the house, work hard, do odd jobs and then take a risk. Sounds simple right?

Well it requires dedication, courage, hard work and some smart work. That is the recipe for success in any profession. Today Walmart is worth 230 billion USD and employs 21 million people! Today Walton family is one of the richest families in the US. His sons run the business. Walmart is one of the reasons of a revolution in the grocery shopping business!

In another such case, Jon Koum, founder of Whats App, was then a 16-year-old Ukrainian Immigrant in California when he started learning programming and hacking. To make ends meet he would sweep floors and collect food stamps. He created something that gave tough competition to the giant Facebook. Mark Zuckerberg then decided to buy it for a whopping 19 billion USD in February 2014.Whether the owner or not, the world will always be thankful to Koum for creating an easy to use communication medium.

Take the example of business tycoon Dhirubhai Ambani, who used to work at a petrol pump to support himself and his family. On weekends, he would set up 'bhajia' stalls to make ends meet. From one small business to another, he explored lot of possibilities and finally started a textile mill in Ahemadabad. Today, The Reliance group of industries employs thousands of people. The net worth of Ambani family is 60 billion USD. Dhirubhai not only overcame odds life threw at him, but also created thousands of jobs. He once said ***"Think big, think fast, think ahead. Ideas are no one's monopoly. You don't need an invitation to start making***

profit."You don't need an invitation to start making profit. Read that twice. Maybe thrice. Let that sink in. Look at the attitude of the man! Here, a lesson we learn from him is to be pro-active. Get up! Start doing something that pays. However small the pay may be, it's important to start somewhere.

We can also see how these people did odd jobs in their difficult times. It's important to understand and believe that no job is too small for you. You should do it if you think it pays you enough and it is not harming anyone. This will also help us develop a right attitude, learn humility. Societal norms have been there for ages and they haven't changed. It's important not to let them consume you or influence your thinking. If you are earning your bread and butter yourself or sponsoring your education yourself or even supporting your family by that little contribution of yours, you should be proud. Proud that you are independent.

When you are successful (which we are sure you will be, touch wood!) you can proudly tell people about the journey that led you there. You will be an inspiration to many.

So my friend at this point of time in your life, you need to stop worrying (actually there's nothing to worry about!) and start working. Life is one tough ride my friend. It's that bump in your way that you're on. You may have thought a million times all the events that led you to this moment in your life. But it's actually of no use. Quit blaming others for your troubles.

Understand that this is not the end of times that this is not how you want to live. Yes, you have made mistakes, you've made some bad decisions, but hey, who hasn't? Every individual out there in the world has done that and a lot of people will do mistakes in the future. You are not freaking perfect and you don't have to be.

The great Albert Einstein wasn't perfect. Poor chap failed math tests in his school life but when he overcame that difficult phase of his childhood, he survived and he made the scariest invention of all times-the nuclear bomb! He made some shocking breakthroughs in science which no one ever thought of! Well you may not be Albert Einstein, but you're definitely not the only one who's failed in life.

Your fate may have knocked you down from your high horse but you definately aren't done yet. It is when you fight this internal battle with your own self that you'll come out of the mess you're in. Put all that happened in your stride. Make a promise to yourself that you'll stop at nothing to make things good. Muster all that internal energy, courage and focus you've got in you. Remember, there's no situation bad enough that can keep you from getting what you want.

There's no problem bad enough you can't get over with. Hang in there my friend for there's nothing that life throws at you that you can't handle. Lose all the fear of failure; shrug off all that negativity that's causing doubts in your mind. Approach all that life throws at you with a clear mind and a never say die attitude. Remember you've got nothing to lose and adopt a fearless approach to life.

You won't see the results immediately, you won't become rich overnight. It'll need constant hard work and perseverance from your end to get the desired results.

Make a serious introspection of your self and your abilities. Make a list of all the things you can do, all your hobbies you like. Make a list of all the contacts in your social circle and keep them ready for your reference.

In situations like these what you need to do is, think out-of-the-box. Well, there are a lot of things you can do to quick buck with. There are some ways of making big bucks and then there are some small ways which will help you survive another day. They say "money attracts money", you have got to put in small bucks if you want to make big bucks.

But let's talk about where these small bucks come from when you don't have them. Let's explore the possibilities of making some money when you don't have any, when you are broke. If you think for a while, you will soon realize that anything that is a "service" to mankind gets paid. You do something that serves the purpose and you will get paid.

That service might require you to have a skill or might just need your time and attention. Look carefully around you, there are lot of jobs that can be created out of this.

There are a lot of jobs for people with every skill. Skills developed for some hobbies can come in handy too. Don't get bogged down if you are from a small town with very limited opportunities. We live in a highly globalized world with everything at the tip of our fingers. Opportunities are nearly countless, you just need to seize them and make the most out of them.

There are skills that get paid such as some offline jobs, freelance coding, mobile app development, graphic design, sound and video editing, translators, etc. Then there are survey websites which need your time and attention for which you get paid.

Now, let's come to the main point. Perhaps the reason why you started reading this book- Ways of making money. There are a lot of them and we encourage only legal ways to do so for obvious reasons. Here we are listing down some mainstream and well-paying ways of making money. We will talk about the jobs which are easy to find irrespective of your age, gender etc. We will talk about all these ways in detail.

Freelancing

Freelancing requires you to have daily access to some facilities like a computer and internet. It may also require some software. Apart from that, you need skills. They may be coding skills, designing skills, fast typing speed, translator (in which case you need to know more than one language fluently), communication skills, etc. There are hundreds of skills that can get you a freelancing job. You just need to look for the right ones according to your skill-set.

There are two ways to look for a freelancing assignment. Find someone you know who can offer you or recommend you for a project offline; for which you need good networking. Sit down and think about all the people you know who can offer you a project. Reach out to them, ask them if they can offer you something. If there's actually something that they think that you can do, they will be more than happy to get you on board. Even their work gets done easily because of you. It's a win-win situation. This is the smoothest way of landing in a job.

But let's talk about another scenario where you don't have any contacts or you don't find a suitable assignment from the ones you know. Worry not! There are hundreds of opportunities available on the internet. So, the first thing to do now is, get yourself registered on freelancing websites. Add your educational details, skill-set, availability and other details. Browse through different websites for some time. Look at the different opportunities available. You might not find anything suitable immediately, be patient. Apply for multiple projects.

Top Freelancing Websites :
1. Toptal (software industry, designers)
2. UpWork (various)
3. 99designs (various)
4. PeoplePerHour (Software industry, digital designers, marketers)
5. localSolo (various)
6. Simplyhired (various)
7. Freelancer (various)

Tips to get better at freelancing:

- Endorse your skills well.
- Update your profile regularly.
- Understand the job.
- Ask questions and be clear about your role.
- Plan ahead. Be pro-active
- Set deadlines for yourself.
- Keep honing your skills.
- Learn a new skill.
- Network well and don't burn the bridges when done with the project.
- Request feedback when done with the assignment.
- Lastly, be professional.
- Always complete the project before deadline.
- Do quality work. Remember quality is more important than quantity. But when you are broke, you got to balance both!

Internships

Internships are not very different from freelancing except that you have to go to the office every day. It is a little more formal and corporate way of working. You will have to work for fixed number of hours every day.

If you are a student studying part time or you get long semester breaks, this is perhaps the best way for you to make some money. You will earn and also end up enhancing your resume. Who knows, you might convert that opportunity into a full time job!

Companies offer internships for two reasons; first, they want to encourage new talent, and second, they don't really want to hire someone full time for a small project. Again, a win-win situation for both. For students doing professional courses, internships can be a game changer. While working with industry professionals, you get to learn lot of new things. You will also be able to get an idea about the career path to be chosen afterwards.

Now let's talk about the important point for us, Money!

Yes, many companies pay really well. The pay may vary depending on skills and number of hours required. Big companies like Google, Microsoft, and Facebook pay as much as $6500-8000 USD/month. These companies however conduct contests to select interns.

Some companies simply post available internships on their websites. Most companies, however, post on online internship searching portals, inviting applications.

Thus, to bag an internship you should be present on these websites. You should register yourself with them adding required details. Also building a good professional profile on LinkdIn can be helpful.

You first need to decide the domain in which you want to intern. The domain maybe something that you have been pursuing a professional degree in (coding, architecture etc.) or a skill-set you have because of your hobbies (creative writing, graphic design etc.) Once you are done with it, start applying for the relevant internships and wait for them to contact you. Remember, Patience!

Top websites for searching internships:

InternShala.com

Letsintern.com

GoAbroad.Org

Idealist.org

Indeed.com

Tips to get internships faster:

Build a strong profile, be authentic.

Write a clear, concise, yet impactful cover letter.

Call the recruiter if you don't receive a reply.

Update your profile regularly.

Ask for feedback .

Look for internships relevant to your skill-set or education.

Be flexible. Remember, you need the money!

Survey Websites

Although this doesn't pay a hefty amount but if you have internet, which I bet you'll find in the neighborhood Starbucks, instead of scrolling mindlessly through Facebook or Instagram feeds you can use it to make a few bucks. Here you get paid for giving your opinions. You are just expected to be honest. It might require you to answer some personal questions. (No, they shouldn't be asking for confidential information such as credit card number or passwords. If you find such questions, do not answer them.)

Some companies conduct market surveys to get an idea about requirements of the customers. Some simply want to make an estimation of production. Some want to improve their products. The best way is to ask a consumer himself about what he wants .It is a fool proof way of doing business and thus, the most popular one now. They study customer behavior, likes/dislikes, needs, tastes etc., to improve their sales.

There are surveys ranging from healthcare, automobile, education to insurance policies. They are studying your behavior through these surveys. So, all you need to do is register yourself on these survey websites. Take surveys. Earn credit points and redeem them. Make sure you know about the redeeming methods beforehand. You don't want to spend hours taking surveys and get a Zara gift card! Make sure you read the feedback about websites before starting survey. You might come across some fake ones. Be alert and smart to identify them.

Again, please do not disclose confidential information at any cost. No website has the right to ask you that. Also avoid signing up by paying an initial amount for registration. You don't want to fall prey to fraudulent activities when you are already broke.

Here are some websites to earn through surveys:

- Toluna
- Swagbucks
- YouGov
- One Pole.
- PopulusLive

Blogging

This method of making money is for the creative / knowledgeable ones with good writing skills. All you need to do is simply present your content in an attractive manner to the readers. Your blog should either give them knowledge / advice or entertain them. How blogging works is this: once you start writing good content and publish it online, people will read it. On the same blogging page, you can place ads or affiliate links. Companies will pay to add these to your content. Thus, more the number of people visiting the websites of these companies more will be your income.

For this, however, you need to have a good number of readers and followers. This will need building viewership through good content. Once you are famous, some offline publications might approach you too.

Topics you can write on
1. Fiction
2. Life lessons/experiences
3. Travel blog
4. Food blog
5. Technology blog
6. Nonfiction /opinions on current issues etc

Tips for successful blogging:
1. Be consistent
2. Do good publicity across social media platforms
3. Invest in good website design
4. Be well informed about the issue and respect critics
5. Make your content simple, easy to understand. Run grammar check.

YouTube videos

Perhaps you are already well aware of this. This is a fun way of money making. But here too, everything depends on the response you get from viewers. If you can make DIY tutorials, Stand-up comedy Acts, review products or simply entertain people by talking, you should try this one.

You need a camera, internet connection and good content for this. When your viewership increases you can start placing ads before or during your videos and you get paid each time someone watches it!

There is catch here. Competition is tough! There are a lot of people out there who have made videos and are waiting for viewership. Your content must be unique for you to succeed.

But if you are creative, there's nothing to worry about. Over time you will figure out a way to make money. You can even turn this into a full-time profession called "YouTuber". How cool is that?!

Here are simple steps to start earning through YouTube (listed on YouTube website:)
1. Login through your Google account
2. Enable your channel for monetization

3. Connect your YOUTUBE channel to an AdSense account in order to EARN money and get paid for your monetized videos.

4. Take a minute to get to know the kind of videos you can monetize with and the different ad formats.

Tips for garnering more views in a short time:

- Do your research: Watch existing videos on the topic you are interested in. Study what most viewed videos offer. Length, speed and visual aspects are very important.
- Once you are done with it, come up with something original.
- Present your video in high audio quality.
- Promote your video on all social media platforms.
- Read feedback you get in the comments section. Respect constructive criticism and work on it.
- Keep your videos as short as possible. Make them entertaining.
- Be consistent. If possible, announce when you will release your next video.

Tutor (online/offline)

Teaching is a noble profession. Apart from helping you earn money, it will teach you a hundred more things. All you need to be a good teacher is to have good communication skills, the ability to illustrate your ideas well and some patience.

In this profession, there is money and then there is the satisfaction you get when someone tells you they know something because of you! It is priceless!

There are two ways of becoming a tutor. You can either gather your students in a room and teach them in person or take online sessions for them. You can also make videos and upload them on online tutoring sites.

Online Tutor:

To become an online tutor, you again need good internet connection and a computer. You need to get yourself registered on websites and you are good to go! In most cases, you will be paid on an hourly basis or module-wise. It again depends on the difficulty level of the content you are teaching. The pay may vary between $5-30 USD/Hours (roughly 300-1800/INR). Over time, as you gain experience, your pay increases.

Websites for online tutors
- Tutor.com
- Vedantu.com
- Teachindia.net
- Chegg
- **Club Z**.
- eTutorWorld
- Khan Academy
- Learn to Be
- Preply
- The Princeton Review
- Revolution Prep

Offline Tutor:

For this you need to contact people who might need tutoring or some coaching/teaching institutes. Let them know about your availability and subjects you are good at. A good academic record in such cases always helps. But if you don't have one, don't worry. If this is something that you think you can do, then you surely can! Offline tuition's maybe for one student or for a group of students and pay varies accordingly. It pays almost as much as online tuition or even more, in some cases. You can surely convert this into a full-time profession.

Mobile App development

If you are a technology geek who is broke, this one is for you! This way of making money can make you a billionaire. Take the example of Jon Koum, Whats App founder.

For this, you need to know mobile app development technology and nothing else! Once you develop the app, put it on Google play-store/iOS App-store and start earning.
There are thousands of apps available on Google play store. Thus, to be successful yours must stand out.
Here are some tips for it:

- Generate a concrete idea through good research.
- Design your app well.
- Keep it simple and user friendly.
- Study the market.
- Have good knowledge about failed apps.
- Update your app from time to time.
- Use social media to promote your product.
- Create something unique, yet useful.

Broker/Estate Agent

If you are someone with excellent networking skills, both on and off internet, you will succeed in making money through this method. Many people around us are selling / renting their houses and shops. There are a large number of people looking for houses or shops. If you can help them find a good deal, you can charge them for your service.

Breaking into this business isn't very difficult. Start with some people you know, who want to sell/buy property. Tell them you will help them find one. Now go to local broker and find something that suits your customer. Of course, the local broker will ask for commission but it's the fastest way to start earning through it. Over time, you can develop your own brand and be a single player in such deals. Even one or two deals a month can pay you a good sum. Plus, it doesn't require you to work every day.

Tips for newbie brokers:
1. Network! Network! Network! Let everyone know you are in the business.
2. Initially keep your fees lower than others to start off.
3. Expand your network to more than one locality.
4. Look for places where lot of real estate properties is being sold / rented out.
5. Create a brand value over time.
6. Be loyal to your customers; help them get a good deal.
7. Do online and offline publicity. Put posters / banners in "market" areas to let people know about you.
8. Make sure the property is legal, do your own research.

Sell your unwanted stuff on eBay / OLX

It may be the hardest thing to do for some people. But it's high time you get rid of those non-productive assets which are so dear to you. Yeah mate, I'm talking about your comic book collection or the action figure collection you've got stuffed in your garage. It's time for a new beginning and this may be the ideal thing to do.

Get rid of all the unnecessary surplus stuff you got stuffed in your house. Old books, extra pair of shoes, some designer merchandise, which has very little use value. Give vanity a break and start thinking practically. Sort out all the stuff in your house into different categories like critical, essential and trash.

Keep all the things you need to make through a day in critical and essential section. The rest obviously gets designated as trash. You need to sell this off. Well this is not a long lasting way to make money because eventually you are going to run out of stuff to sell. But for the time being you can make some money out of it. Find buyers in your neighbourhood or sell them off on online platforms like:

1. EBay.com.
2. Quickr.com
3. ThredUp.com (For kids clothing)

4. amazon.com/sellyourstuff.   (Selling books)
5. Glyde.com.   (ipad, iphone, ipod or Video Games)
6. REBELLE. (Designer bags and shoes)
7. Vinted
8. Vide dressing
9. craigslist
10. chairish.   (unique or designer homeware, as well as antiques and jewellery)
11. offerup

Tips to sell your stuff quickly:

1. Present your product well.
2. Give proper and true information about its age size, usage etc.
3. Add good quality unedited pictures.
4. Do a little research about pricing beforehand.
5. Price your product reasonably. Don't keep it too high. Don't sell it too cheap either.

Create websites

This can be an ideal job for a student who has done an IT professional course .You get paid for creating and maintaining websites. With almost all the businesses going online, everyone wants to have a website of their own to create brand value. This is where you get one more chance of earning money.

A whole lot of platforms are available for website creation depending on the content and complexity of design. Nowadays, most stores need a website to keep up with the fast-growing culture of online shopping. Various online resources have made the task of website creation easy. Most of these platforms have templates to cater to the demand of the user. These platforms have removed the previously needed exhaustive scripting in PHP and html. Of course, you need to know those scripting languages to provide customers with some unique requirements, but that's a rare case.

These platforms include

1. Google sites
2. WordPress
3. Yola

4. Webs.com
5. Wix.com
6. Namecheap.com
7. GoDaddy.com
8. Shopify.com
9. Hostgator.com
10. Site123.com
11. Squarespace.com
12. Networksolutions.com
13. Ionos.com
14. SquareOnline.com

Tax filing

With a lot of tax reforms happening, people with an accounting background have a lot of opportunities. With the advent of new taxation policies, this is definitely a way to make a quick buck. Students studying in colleges can definitely help some people not familiar with modern technology.

If you have good experience in taxation and financial laws, you can definitely make a lot of money acting as a consultant for a small-time firm because they usually cannot afford to have permanent employees to file taxes once a year.

You can also work as an online tax consultant and offer your services to people. This isn't very difficult. The steps for tax filing are listed on the websites. You just need to follow them. Make sure the tax is calculated by an authorised Chartered Accountant.

Valet attendant

This is definitely a very simple option to make some money. The tips would be an added bonus too. All you need is a class C driver's licence and some neat social skills to get hired. Valet attending requires a certain stamina and endurance, as there is perpetual movement of the attendant in bringing vehicles and/or articles to and from patrons for hours on end. Valet attendant must be able to perform under pressure in order to meet the customer's time constraints, as well as give an orderly and timely appearance while retrieving vehicles. You must be polite, attentive and responsible to fulfil a client's needs. The job comes with an added advantage. You get to drive the latest cars and supercars on a regular basis. Now who'd say no to that!

Old age Care

They say old age is a second childhood. But hey! There's your window of opportunity. You can help old people staying alone do their daily chores like buying veggies and running errands. A lot of the elderly people join old age care and communities just so that they have someone to share their lives with, someone to have fun with. If you serve the elderly people in your neighbourhood you'll definitely earn some money. More than that, you'll get solid doses of wisdom from these experienced people and that will always come in handy. You may come across lots of folks suffering from Alzheimer's or dementia. Such people need a lot of help and care. The important quality to have while doing such a job is to be patient and understanding and anticipating a person's needs. Make the most of the opportunity to serve these folks. You never know they may just remember a best buddy who owns a MNC who owes them a favour! After all service to man is service to God. And we all know the lord works in mysterious ways!

Babysitter

This is by far the best profession for college girls and women to earn some good money. The demands of this profession are quite high given that the number of working women and men is increasing day by day. Maternity leaves are getting shorter and shorter with women getting back to work as soon as possible to not fall back career wise. People thus hire nannies to look after their children. Now this profession will need you to work anywhere from 6 hours a day to as much as 15-16 hours a day.On an average it pays around $5-15 USD/Hour in western countries where as around 250-2500 Rs/Day in India. This job requires you to have patience with kids, get through their cranky moods, change diapers, and force-feed them. But it can also be quite entertaining when the kids are in a good mood and you get paid for playing with them!

Lawn trimming

People love to have lush green lawns on their property to see from their porch. But not many people can actually take care of it. People from the upper middle class hardly find time to attend to such chores. This gives you a chance to step in. You can maintain lawns for such people and make some easy cash out of it. Maybe you can even extend your services to gardening. Taking care of plants is a very important for them to grow properly. There's also the scope of further expansion of this gig into a full-time profession. Since maintenance of lawns and plants is a regular task, you can earn on a regular basis.

Photographer

If you have a good background in photography and content creation you may work as a photographer for magazines, websites and even social events. Students can also take up this job if they've got good photography skills, which is a very popular trait in today's kids. In an effort to get maximum likes and comments on their photos they end up clicking amazing photographs which may envy even the best pros out there. So, if you've got that creative instinct and drive, you can make some serious dough from it.

To get started with this you can either sign yourself up with a photography/modelling agency or start from social media. Platforms like nstagram are a great launch pad for a career in this field.

Subject X

This may sound desperate, but clinical trials and experimental medicine need a lot of people belonging to all types of races, ages and backgrounds to test their research. You can get paid reasonably well. There's obviously a risk, but FDA regulations and norms make sure that all safeguards and checks are done prior to human testing. Look at it this way; you can be a contributor to science and the future of technology.

Also, a lot of ergonomic research is done during product development stage in companies. You can offer your services there too and get paid for your suggestions and opinions.

Car washing

The constantly hectic and mind-numbing schedule of some people can make them forget about their ever-reliable Chevy. For these folks, money is not an object, but time is. They hardly get the time to clean their cars. You can cater to their needs and provide special services for the super busy folks.

Catering services

College kids can surely make this gig a source of constant cash. These kinds of jobs demand less working hours and are mostly available during weekends and special occasions. You can come into contact with people with a lot of temp-job experience and they can definitely be a good source of information regarding new opportunities for short time and quick money.

Laundry Services

Laundry services such as washing, ironing clothes is a very high paying part time job.You need to know how to operate a washing machine and you need to know how to operate the iron ! Also, the job is going to be there all year around. In India, you get 15-20rs/cloth for washing where as 5-8 rs/cloth for ironing. Even doing 30-50 of them in a day will pay you enough to support yourself. In America, they charge by the pound or articles each for ironing and pressing of clothes. Prices range from $5 a pound to $3 each piece for suits coats, shirts, ties, and dress clothing.

Tourist Guide

If you live near a tourist spot, it's time to cash in on the advantage and make a real deal out of it. Every tourist craves for information from local people. No amount of travel guides and history books can talk about a place like a son of the soil can. Tourists enjoy old legends and stories about a place. You are bound to make a lot of money in this gig if you are a good presenter and storyteller.

Be clear and dynamic and add your own natural flavours. There's a lot of scope to have a regular income if you tie up with a travel agency and touring groups. If you are really great at your job then you can permanently shift to this as your career choice and join tour companies where you can get a lot to learn, earn and at the same time have loads of fun!
To make it easily accessible, you should have enlisted yourself on local state tourism boards.

This job is not just about making money. You end up representing your culture and your heritage. If you know any foreign languages you certainly have an advantage over your peers. People having a background in media and showbiz can take it to the next level in terms of presentation and content delivery.

Deliver newspaper, pizzas, groceries, foods, and more

Do you know how often an average person eats pizza? Americans alone eat approximately 100 acres of pizza a day! There are approximately 61,269 pizza outlets in America!

These astonishing numbers indicate one thing that no matter how you are, who you are or where you are from, a famished individual thinks of pizza 9 times out of 10. The reason being, their variety, taste and, of course, the timely delivery services.

You can definitely try your hand at these jobs as they demand good driving skills and some shrewd customer interactions. Same can be said about the burger outlets as well. These people really do work on a war footing to make our lives easy. So prompt and "need for speed" style people are really needed here! Cutting through urban traffic should be definitely on your resume to get this opportunity.

It's a great way to network as well. People really do remember a person and care enough for a person who answers the cry of their tummy! With recent developments in modes of needs (Pandemic quarantines and lockdowns) food delivery is among one of the most needed jobs around.

There are a lot of opportunities to be a newspaper delivery man as well. It's just a morning job and effectively opens up a lot for time to accommodate a few other gigs later in your day too.

Services like DoorDash, GrubHub, Uber Eats, have surfaced and become one of the most needed services of the day. When it comes to the best food delivery services, it boils down to a choice between Grubhub and Seamless — the two services are run by the same company and are essentially interchangeable — or Doordash. We think Grubhub's support of multiple payment options gives it a slight edge, though DoorDash has a lot going for it, too.If you're already using

Uber to get around town, the Uber Eats app will have a familiar interface for ordering meals to go. Several other food delivery options specialize in certain areas. InstaCart lets you order from grocery stores, while services such as Delivery.com and GoPuff include snacks and drinks among other household items that they'll bring to your door. If you don't mind picking up your own food, ChowNow lets you place to-go orders at a variety of local eateries in your area.

With social distancing guidelines forcing some people to stay indoors, several apps have added options that let you specify where food deliveries can be dropped off so that you and your driver can stay 6 feet apart at all times. We've noted which food delivery services have added contact-free delivery options.

Bug Finder

If you've worked in the software testing and networking domain, it's a very good opportunity to earn some hard cash by finding critical bugs in websites and apps. There are very generous rewards for finding the flaws in the security of a website or an app. Major software companies like Google, Facebook, Twitter have their own programs to ensure their products are secure. Google has the Vulnerability Reward Program, Facebook has Bug Bounty program and so on. Sometimes people have managed to bag great jobs due to the recognition and fame these things offer.

Election Campaigns

Every election campaign brings a lot of jobs and opportunities for temps and freelancers. Varied activities like funding, publicity, voter research, data analysts and campaign organisers need a lot of man power and skilled individuals from all possible backgrounds. A lot of work goes on while managing funds and their disbursement, so people from accounting background are required too.

Doing Assignments and Projects

Every class has a kid with lots of cash and negligible will to work hard on projects and assignments. It's not that hard to spot such people and enter into a mutually beneficial gig with them. These chances are also a regular thing given the nature of academic work load. People in engineering colleges often get a considerably large amount of mediocre assignments and drawing sheets.

You can make good money from such arrangements. The money you're offered increases exponentially as the submission dates approach!

Virtual Assistants

With the advent of social media platforms and the dramatic expansion of all communication channels, there has been tremendous demand for people who can answer your emails, sifting out the most important communiques. Often, writers, actors and professionals popular in the mainstream media need a virtual assistant who can work off site and make their life easy by taking care of their fan mail and make some timely appointments and scheduling tasks. This can be a well rewarding job and would open a lot of opportunities for you in the future by virtue of the contacts you establish.

Consultant

You can always bank on the experience of your last job and act as a consultant in the domain that you excel in. You can act as a Marketing consultant or a Public Relations Consultant for firms and individuals. There's a lot of demand for people working on contract basis and offering good quality services at competitive prices.

Security Guard

Are you a real beefy guy or a gym freak? Do you have an intimidating personality? Then brace this opportunity. All you'll have to do is stand tall and keep the nuisance out of your sight. Break some fights and make sure you have a tight grip on situations that may transpire into fights or even worse.

You may even join a security agency as a bodyguard. A martial arts course can definitely improve your prospects.

Makeup artist

Even though there's more demand for women in this profession, the market is opening up for men as well. People nowadays are more conscious about their appearance and are ready to invest good amount of money and time in self-grooming.

Thus, a constant demand for makeup artists is there. You get paid on an hourly basis for this. It's not very difficult to learn to do makeup.Its all out there on the internet. Start with people you know and you will slowly grow your business.You can also start working in beauty parlours on a part time basis.

Masseuse

If you have that magic in your hands to soothe pain from a tense body its time you put it to good effect. Though you can't work as a professional masseuse you can definitely provide services to your friends and family and charge them on an hourly basis. Through referrals and word of mouth publicity, you can grow your reputation and end up becoming a pro.

Gym trainer

If you gym/exercise regularly you can consider this an option too. Awareness about fitness is at its all time peak these days. Lot of people want to go to the gym to lose weight /gain weight, improve stamina, build muscles and what not. In developed countries and urban areas, a lot of people are signing up for gym membership. Business is flourishing and a lot of new gyms are opening up.

This is where employment opportunity is created. You can become a gym trainer. You have to teach people about different exercises and make sure they do it right. You have to motivate them to slog harder and push their limits. That's all. You can work full day or for a few hours a day and get paid quite a decent sum for this.

Swimming Instructor

If you know swimming, you have one more option to earn money. Apply to your nearest swimming coaching center and you are good to go! Zero capital investment! It usually only takes a few hours from your schedule (sometime in the morning and then in the evening), plus you get to practice swimming everyday for free. You can manage well with the money you make out of it.

Extra

Drama companies and entertainment industry are not always in the search of superstars. They need normal people like you and me to fill that void behind the lead actor. Yeah you got it right. There are numerous opportunities for all kind of artists who can feature in a little TV show or a film. Mostly paid on an hourly wage basis, it's a good opportunity to make some money while getting your mojo back and raise the fallen spirits! Who doesn't like to be on TV!

Cook

If you've got the fine talent of making people lick their fingers you can never be unemployed. Whatever the economic, political or social conditions are, people never stop eating!

And very few people really know their way around a kitchen. If you've got those fine culinary skills, time to put them to use! You don't need to be a chef for that. You can sell home made cookies, lasagna or sell some barbecue! You can always make use of your house for cooking and deliver the goods to your customers. You know the guy who started KFC started the same way!

There's a lot of demand for home made lunch/dinner cities the world over. So, there are a lot of ways you can make money by cooking.

Cab Driver

You can work for the upcoming cab hiring companies like Ola, Uber etc. and make good money. You'd require a car and a driving license for that. You can make use of those well polished driving skills of yours. There are some technical and legal formalities, but that won't be an issue if you are an upstanding citizen with a clean record.

Bartender

Yeah man. Time to mix those juices and shove worries off your mind by providing some great bar service. You don't need to be a trained mixologist to make a Dirty Martini! A few YouTube videos and a bit of practice can teach you that. You can definitely up your game by some chit-chatting skills. Remember nothing sells wine better than a spirited bartender. Drinking is a favourite pastime around the world. So a shot of encouragement is what your customers need!

Farming

If you live in a rural area this can be a good bet for your time. Farming requires a lot of man power. You can learn the skills in no time. A minor demonstration is all you need. You can be a labourer earning on a daily basis. Nowadays with advancement in technology, some farming jobs require you to only operate the farm equipments.But yeah you need to be ready to get yourself dirty and put all your muck-related insecurities at bay!

Modelling

A curvaceous or a muscular body is always an asset. You can model for a small time agency or an advertisement. Opportunities are always there with ad-commercials and small designers. You can make a real career out if it as well. You need to find your employers online or audition for the job. Getting a good photo-shoot done and creating a portfolio will help you get a job sooner.

Bounty Hunter

If you've got some law enforcement experience then this can be a very good opportunity for you to put your skills to work. Of course there'll be a few agonizing experiences due to the lack of a badge, but if you really have a skill to join the dots, then this can be the perfect thing for you to do. You shouldn't do this just for playing Sherlock, because this might not be the job for amateurs and hobbyists.

Packers and Movers

This can be a very good gig for making a quick buck. People move around all the time. You can make use of that real estate agent friend for yours for information on such people and help them to pack and move their stuff. You'll find all the packing stuff in any supermarket and need a truck for moving out the stuff. If you have a big SUV then it certainly can be a very economical option for you.

So that's it folks! Till now we have listed more than 30 ways of earning money. Some need your skills; some need your time, while some need emotional maturity and availability. Pick one and get going. Soon you will start earning and stop being broke. We congratulate you in advance for that!

There are hundreds of ways of making money and we have only listed a few of them. There are ones which are easy to find and pay you well. Let me tell you there are certainly a lot many things you and I can do. You take a look around and you will find some more.

All you need is to look with the intent of finding a job. Once you get started you will surely get better with time. You won't need me to tell you how to increase your income. Apart from supporting yourself you are going to get a once in a lifetime kind of experience. You are going to meet some good people and some bad ones. Carry gratitude for the former and ignorance for the latter!

Making money last longer....

Earning money is only a job half done. To make it last longer is another aspect which you need to focus on. By this time you must have figured out that one of the reasons why you are broke is because you spent unwisely. That expensive toy / gadget just to get the feeling of being cool, that party you threw just to have fun with your friends, those eating habits in expensive restaurants instead of cooking your food, renting an apartment bigger than what you need, spending lot of cash on fuel while all you do is roam around in the city just to pass your time, paying thousands of bucks to listen to your favourite rock band or watch a football match.

All of that have contributed to where you are today.

If you look around, you will find that one of the reasons rich people have money is that they spend wisely. They live simply. Cut down on expenses. For example,Founder of Zara Amancio Ortega is one of the richest people in Spain. But he lives in a simple apartment building,wears simple clothes and leads a simple life. Lot of billionaires do the same. They enjoy their work so much that they don't need other ways to have fun.

They have a minimalist approach towards their lives. They are no doubt good at earning money ,but they are also good at saving it. So now you need to change your lifestyle a bit. You need to think twice before making a purchase. You should always ask yourself one question before buying anything "what difference will it make if I don't buy this? "If you can't find a good answer to this question you know what to do.

Step out of the store! This is not the time to buy things for luxury. No matter how much you want it; there are more essential things to buy.

Here's a tip about how you can save while doing monthly grocery shopping: Before going to the shop, make a list of all that you are going to need; and when in the store, head straight to those sections. This will help you avoid making unwanted purchases like candies and cold drinks. While making the grocery list, divide them into three categories; vital, essential and desired.

Grains, milk, sugar and sprouts, all come in the vital category. You need to eat daily and thus you must buy them. Stuff such as bread,tea,coffee are essential, you can eliminate some of them to cut down on your expenses. Cold drinks, chocolates chips are desired by all of us but you cant afford them. Remember you are trying to make a living and you are broke!

All we can tell you at moment is hang in there. Do not let negative thoughts crowd your mind. Please do not harm yourself / get into wrong addictions no matter how bad life seems to be. It is going to get better.

Remember, like everything else, this too shall pass. As time passes you will realize how efficient you have become in managing your money. While you are cutting down on fun invest your time in yourself. Read books,learn a new skill.

At the end, the feeling of empowerment that you get when you start supporting yourself can not be described in words. You are brave to have taken this decision to support yourself. Now all you need is to take the initiative.

In the future, when you look back at this phase you will have tons of memories Also, you never know you can also discover the best full time profession for you!

The world is your canvas and you are the artist! Paint it the way you want. Make sure that this time you make that painting vibrant enough. Make sure you add the colors of hardwork, determination and positivity. Make sure you make it a masterpiece, a masterpiece that everyone will adore; everyone will look up to YOU whenever they hit a rough patch.

Make sure you mesmerize and enthrall everyone with this piece of yours. I'm quite sure that captivating colours and natural strokes in your piece will be an immaculate portrayal of your frivolous courage and tremendous fortitude. You ensure that you convince and inspire people watching it, that there's absolutely no room for failure if you're willing to put in those hard yards.

In the battle of life, no one escapes unscathed. There's always a collateral damage. What happened to you was just that! Now, take a step back, regroup, re-evaluate your position, re- strategize your move and make that assault, that final, brutal,vengeful assault and win all that you want. You'll achieve your goal ultimately.

You'll get all that wounded pride and dignity back. You'll get what you always desired. Yeah there'll be battle scars, there'll be some agonizing memories, but when you get that taste for the good life it'll all be a memory, an inspiring story.

After the storm has passed and the dust has settled there'll come a much awaited tranquility and stability. All the best for the journey you are about to embark on!
We hope your tough times end very soon.

About the Author

Robert Cunningham is an author, editor, proofreader, and owner of Khinsharri Publishing. He has several books published, three cookbooks to date, as well as seeing several friends published through his businesses.

An avid Science Fiction fan, he also is the leader of an international fan club, Star Trek based and has numerous Facebook pages worldwide in such diverse places as Italy, Iceland, Russia, Brazil, Canada, Australia, Sweden, the UK, Scotland, Germany, and several across America.

As a family man, he has a wife of almost 16 years, and between them they share 11 children, 14 grandchildren, and 9 great grandchildren, spread across the country far and wide. Currently residing in Kansas, he has taken up residency on a small town more suited to a quieter life and the pursuit of writing more and more.